ELLA
Diaries

TOP
SECRET!

AF585361

With thanks to Robyn English and the Nature Protectors from Rolling Hills PS—Alicia, Malia, Abbey, Chloe, Genevieve, Elle, Forum, Claire and Victoria—M.C.

For my nephews, Jordan, Jack and Alex—D.M.

Scholastic Australia
An imprint of Scholastic Australia Pty Limited
PO Box 579 Gosford NSW 2250
ABN 11 000 614 577
www.scholastic.com.au

Part of the Scholastic Group
Sydney • Auckland • New York • Toronto • London • Mexico City
• New Delhi • Hong Kong • Buenos Aires • Puerto Rico

Published by Scholastic Australia in 2017.

A catalogue record for this book is available from the National Library of Australia

ISBN: 9781760279059

Typeset in Sweetie Pie.

Printed in China by Hang Tai Printing Company Limited.

Scholastic Australia's policy, in association with Hang Tai, is to use papers that are renewable and made efficiently from wood grown in responsibly managed forests, so as to minimise its environmental footprint.

10 9 8 7 6 5 4 23 24 / 1

# ELLA Diaries

## Monday, before dinner

Dear Diary,

I am SOOOO EXCITERED!

This morning at school assembly, Mr Martini (our extremely excellent school principal) announced that something VERY, VERY SPECIAL is going to happen. Right here at our very own school!

I LOVE it when VERY, VERY SPECIAL things happen. Especially if they happen to me!

And guess what the VVST* is?

HINT: It starts with these letters:

* VVST = Very, very special thing.

If you said any of these things you would be **WRONG, WRONG, WRONG.**

The **VVST** is that we are all going to be

Only we don't have to protect the **WHOLE** planet all at once. That would just be **WEIRD**. Mr Martini said we can do small things every day to help the environment, right here at our school!

Like getting our school grounds looking beautiful by planting flowers,

and making our own compost to put on the garden beds,

and picking up litter. We're even going to have competitions each week to see which class collects the most! And that class can win fantabulous prizes!

Mr Martini said there's also going to be a **VERY SPECIAL JOB** for a **VERY SPECIAL PERSON!**

(I wonder what it could be?)

???!

Then about 900 kids (including me) all started waving their hands in the air, wanting to ask questions.

But Mr Martini said our teachers would tell us more about how the program works when we're back in class.

**YESSSSS!**

Have to go now, Dad's calling me for dinner. I'll tell you the rest later on tonight!

Love,

Ella xx

## Monday night, late (in bed, when I am supposed to be asleep)

I'm back! Sorry it took so long. Max wanted me to read him a bedtime story. THREE TIMES! With actions! And funny voices!

Bedtime STORY

So, there we all were, sitting in class working away quietly on our Endangered Animals of the World projects,* when Ms Weiss said to pack everything away so she could tell us more exciting things about our new Planet Protector Program.

* I am doing whales for my project, which are my third most favourite type of animal after dogs and praying mantises.

And guess what? Ms Weiss said there are lots more planet protectoring things we can do at home as well as at school!

# WAYS WE CAN HELP PROTECT OUR PLANET

## 3 GROW your own FOOD!

## 4 Help to save endangered ANIMALS!

## 5 Walk to SCHOOL in a walking BUS!

And guess what else we can do?

Bring NUDE FOOD from home for our lunch!

When Ms Weiss said 'Nude Food', Peter and Raf and all the other boys started laughing like hyenas and slapping each other's arms and whispering stupid things like 'Oooooooo' and 'Heh heh' and 'Nudie rudie' to each other.

Hee... ha

ha ha ha

Bleuchhh.

Boys are SOOOO ~~immachewer~~ immature.

So then Ms Weiss had to explain to them that **Nude Food** is food that is

a) chopped off from **BIGGER** bits of food, or

b) wrapped up in its own skin, or

c) made at home by you.

And then you bring it to school in a special lunchbox with sweet little compartments.

UN-Nude Food is all wrapped up in planet-destroying plastic wrapping.

It is NOT food without any clothes on. That would just be WEIRD.

Ms Weiss waited patiently until the boys had stopped whispering and arm slapping and giggling like hyenas and were sitting up straight properly in their seats again. And then she told us something really, really, REALLY excitering.

It's about the **SPECIAL JOB** Mr Martini was talking about!

There is going to be an election to choose a

**PLANET PROTECTOR CAPTAIN**

who will be in charge of all the planet-protecting projects at school. And if you're in Grade 5 or 6 —like we are!—you can try out for it.

Ms Weiss said the PPC (Planet Protector Captain) gets to do really importerant **aMAZing** and **EXcellent** things, like making special speeches at assembly. And teaching the teensy tiny kids about how to be good planet protectors.

Dressed up like a superhero in a special superhero outfit!!!

Zow-ee! I've always wanted to ~~wear a superhero outfit~~ be a superhero! I can do really cool ninja moves, just like superheroes do.

AND I love EVERYTHING about nature. Especially animals. And flowering plants. And animals that live on flowering plants, like praying mantises.

praying mantis

When Ms Weiss had finished talking, Zoe (my BFF) gave me a little nudge with her elbow and looked at me with shiny eyes.

Shiny eyes

Then she whispered, 'You could do it, Ella.'

And I whispered back, 'Do what?'

And she said, 'Be the Planet Protector Captain. You'd be **PERFECT** for it.'

And then I gave Zoe a little nudge back with my **OWN** elbow, and looked back at her with even **SHINIER** eyes.

In fact, our eyes were so shiny, they were like two sets of twin suns, ~~ilumernating~~ ~~alluminating~~ lighting up all the planets in the universe! Especially the ones that need protectoring.

And I said, 'So could you!'

But guess what? Zoe said she'd already had a go at being importerant when she had a really, really, really BIG main role in the school play. (And I didn't, even though I really, really, REALLY wanted the exact same role. ☹)

And then Zoe said now it was **MY** turn to be the importerant one. And that I should absolutely, definitely, positively try out to be the PPC.

(This is why Zoe is my BBFF.*)

* Best Best Friend Forever.

I was just about to put my hand up and let Ms Weiss know that I would be absolutely, positively, completely **PERFECT** for the PP Captain job when . . .

Somebody else beat me to it.

And guess who it wa

s?

Oops. Mum just came in and gave me a talking-to about still having my light on when I'm supposed to be asleep.
I had to quickly hide you under the doona so she couldn't see what I was doing.

I'll write more in the morning, I promise!

Good night,

E x

## Tuesday morning, very, very early

Dearest Diary,

It took me FOREVER to get to sleep last night. I kept thinking of more and more ideas for planet protecting. (I got up to Idea #327! Some of them are REALLY excellent!)

#327...

So anyway, the beatering person who got to talk to Ms Weiss first was: Peach Parker. The most annoying, irritating, pestiferous, pesky person in the history of annoying, irritating, pestiferous, pesky ~~persons~~ people.

In fact, Peach is so pesky that other pesky creatures—like bitey mosquitoes and sting-y bull ants—RUN when they see her coming.

After Peach put her hand up Ms Weiss said, 'Yes, Peach?'

And Peach said, 'I'm SOOO happy we're going to be doing a planet protecting program, Ms Weiss. Protecting the planet is SOOO worthwhile and important.'

**Bleuchhh.**

I jiggled my hand around and around in the air like a jiggling windmill. But Ms Weiss didn't even notice me.

She was too busy smiling at Peach. ☹

Peach gave her a big smile back. And then she told Ms Weiss that she had GAZILLIONS of excellent ideas for how to protect the planet. And that she couldn't WAIT to get started.

And guess what? Ms Weiss smiled at her AGAIN! The type of smile she gives someone when she's about to write their name on the board under the 'STUDENT STARS' heading.

And then something horrendous happened.

Ms Weiss told Peach that having all those wonderful ideas meant she would make an **Excellent** Planet Protector Captain. And that she hoped she was thinking of going in the election for it, because she was sure Peach would get **LOTS** of votes.

Princess Peach sat up very straight in her seat and smiled around royally with a big sneery smirk on her face, like she'd won the election already.

~~DOUBLE~~ **TRIPLE Bleuchhh.**

**It is SO NOT FAIR!**

It should have been me telling Ms Weiss about all **MY** excellent planet protectering ideas. And then Ms Weiss telling **ME** that I would make an excellent Planet Protector Captain, and about all the votes I'd get if I went in the election.

BUTTERFLY GARDEN

Idea #216

I was just about to put my hand up again and tell her all about one of my excellent ideas—Idea #216: Making a Butterfly Garden in your Bedroom—when the bell went for the end of school.

Talk more tomorrow, Diary.

Love,

Ella xx

## Tuesday, straight after school

Dear Diary,

Zoe and I walked to school together this morning like we always do. And Zoe was just telling me some interesting facts about mountain gorillas (the animal she is doing for her Endangered Species of the World project), when I noticed three girls from Grade 2 standing at the school gates.

ZOE

Mountain Gorilla

And they were wearing matching green T-shirts with letters on the front. Like this:

And they were handing out things from a big box to everyone as we came through the gates.

And guess what the things were?

YESSSSSSSSSSS! I **LOVE** glitter pens. Especially mauve ones.

I was just turning my glitter pen over to see if it was a Glitterama one (my favourite brand) when I noticed a bright green sticker stuck to the other side.

And guess what it said?

Zoe's glitter pen had a sticker saying PP 4 PP on it too. And so did Cordelia's. And Amethyst's. And my second-best friend, Chloe's. And her best friends Poppy's and Georgia's. And all the other kids' who were walking through the gate.

I wonder what it means???????

Bye for now.
Yours 4 ever,
Ella

## Wednesday, after dinner

Dear Diary-doo,

Something really WEIRD is going on.

Zoe and I were walking through the school gates again this morning and I was just telling her how a whale's tongue weighs as much as a whole elephant when a big group of little first-grade kids ran past, squealing their heads off.

And guess why they were squealing?

Their tiny little-kid arms were full of lollies! And they couldn't wait to get them to their play area so they could stuff them into their squealerous mouths!

And then one of the little kids crashed into another little kid. And their lollies went flying everywhere.

So Zoe picked one of them up. (A lolly. Not a little kid.)

And guess what was stuck to the back of it?

A green sticker.
Saying PP 4 PP.

What does it all mean, Diary?

E x

## Thursday, after school

Dear Diary,

I am SHOCKED.

That is all.

Ella

## Thursday, about twenty minutes later, after a nice soothing bowl of chocolate ice-cream (with double caramel topping) (and sprinkles)

OK, I'm ready to write about what happened now.

This morning when Zoe and I arrived at school there were giganterous green balloons ballooning above the gates. Everyone was standing around pointing and staring at them.

And guess what was written on them?

You're right.

And then Amethyst arrived. And Cordelia. And Chloe and Georgia and Poppy. So we all got into a little huddle and tried to figure out what all those Ps on the glitter pens and the lollies and the balloons stood for.

Here are some of our guesses and chances of being right:

| Guesser | Guess | Chance |
|---|---|---|
| CORDELIA | Purple Pigs 4 Puzzling Plans | 0% |
| AMETHYST | Playful Pixies 4 Precious Palaces | 0% |
| Chloe | Popular Panthers 4 Prying Princesses | 0% |
| POPPY | Panicky Pockets 4 Posh Peas | 0% |
| GEORGIA | Peaceful Pillows 4 Perky Pirates | 0% |
| ZOE | Pink Pencils 4 Pesky People | 0% |
| ME | Picky Peanuts 4 Perfect Pets | 0% |

But none of these made even a TINY bit of sense.

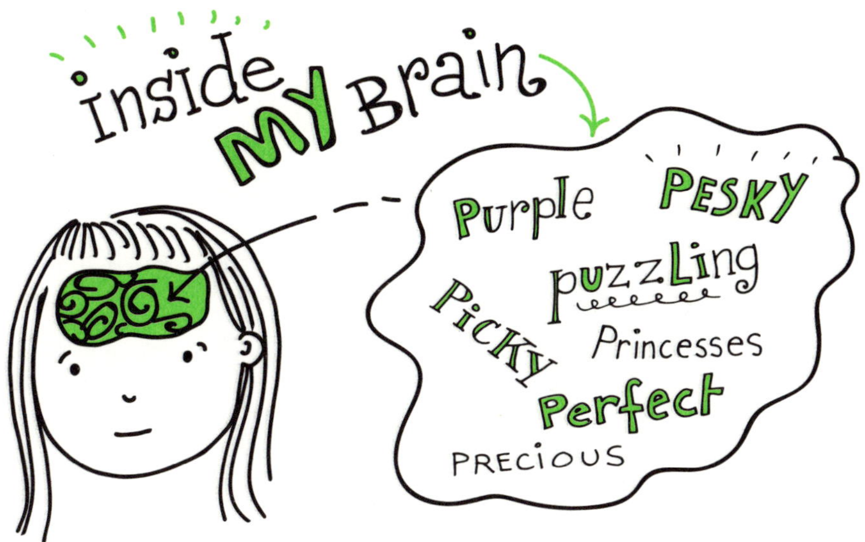


We were just deciding these were all WRONG, WRONG, WRONG and that we were hopelessly hopeless at guessing.

And then we saw a giganterous poster stuck to the wall outside the girls' toilets.

All of a sudden one of those cartoon light bulbs went PING in my brain.

Here's what we all said next:

**Me** (excitedly): I know what the letters mean!
**Zoe** (excitedlier): Me too!
**Everyone else** (excitedliest): What?!?
**Me**: Well, the first PP stands for Peach Parker.
**Zoe**: And the last PP stands for Planet Protector.
**Me**: And the 4 just means 'for'.
**Everyone else**: Peach Parker for Planet Protector!

Amethyst (sighing): It sounds like she's trying to get everyone to vote for her.

Cordelia (shiny-eyed): Of course! The lollies. And the glitter pens. And the giganterous balloons. And this poster. They're all part of her election campaign. She's trying to make everyone like her so they'll vote for her to be the Planet Protector Captain.

Me: NOOOOOOOOOOOOo!!!

Zoe and I ran madly around the school grounds like mad things, on the hunt for more of Peach's posters.

And guess what? They were EVERYWHERE!

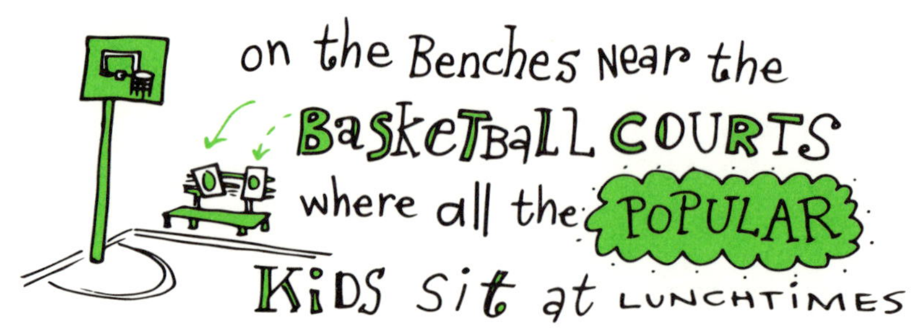


Everything was looking hopelessly hopeless. I was just about to dissolve into teeny tiny little pieces of desperating despair and float away into nothingness . . .

when Zoe had one of her BRILLIANT ideas.

Ha!

So I quickly called an Emergency Campaign Meeting (ECM) after school.

Have to go now, Diary. Zoe will be on her way. And I haven't got the snacks ready or put up the 'KEEP OUT!' sign* on my bedroom door yet!

EMERGENCY CAMPAIGN MEETING **in PROGRESS**

Only people in **GRADE** 5 and UP

~~ALOUD~~ AllOWED

* This is to stop people like my little sister Olivia coming in and stealing our snacks or blabbing all our business to the WRONG PEOPLE.

I'll tell you EVERYTHING about what happened after our meeting.

Yours 4 ever,

E

## Thursday night, in bed

Dear Diary,

We had our ECM. And it was aMAZing! (Mostly.)

First of all we ate all the snacks. (Except for one that fell on the floor and got scooped up by Bob before I could rescue it.)

Then I had a big argument with Olivia. Here's what happened:

**Sound effects**: Knock, knock, knock!

**Bob**: WOOF!

**Zoe** (helpfully): There's someone at the door, Ella.

**Me** (casually): No there isn't.

**Sound effects** (louderer): **KNOCK, KNOCK, KNOCK!!!**

**Bob** (agitatedly): **WOOF! WOOF!**

**Zoe** (firmly): There is too someone at the door. Even Bob can hear them.

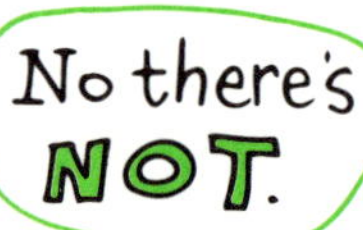


**Me** (firmlier): No there isn't. It's just a ~~figmet~~ figment of your imagination. And also Bob's.

Zoe: But–

Olivia (muffled): **EL-LAAA! open the DOOR and let ME in!**

Me: GO AWAY.

Olivia (still muffled): I'm going to tell Mum on you. And then you'll be in BIG trouble.

Me: No I won't. Can't you read? The sign says 'Only Grade 5 and up allowed'.

Olivia: What sign?

Me (sighing): The SIGN ON THE DOOR.

Olivia: Huh? There IS no sign on the door.

Me (getting up and opening the door so I can show it to her): See? Anyone with even a tiny brain could–

Olivia (scooting through the door into my room and cuddling up on my bed next to Bob before I could stop her): Hehehe. Tricked you!

Me: ☹

Sometimes Olivia makes me so mad I want to scream. Like this:

And then Olivia said something horribly horrendous. So horribly horrendous I can barely write it down. But I will try.

WARNING: SHOCKED ALERT.

She said, 'If you don't let me stay, I won't vote for you to be Planet Projector Captain. And I'll tell all the rest of my class not to vote for you to be Planet Projector Captain either! So there.'

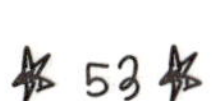

I was **SHOCKED**. And so was Zoe. How did she even know???

I was just about to tell Olivia to leave my room ~~IMEEDIATLY~~ ~~IMMEEDIETLY~~ straight away and never ever **EVER** come back, and it's not even called a Planet **PROJECTOR** Captain anyway, when she looked at me with big puppy dog eyes and said, 'Please, please, **PLEEEEEEEEASE** can I stay?'

And so did Bob. (Look at me with puppy dog eyes, I mean. **NOT** say, 'Pleeeeeeeease'. That would just be WEIRD.)

So I decided to let Olivia stay. But only if she promised to keep quiet and not annoy us by asking stupid questions or touching any of my stuff.

And then Zoe and I did my campaign plan.

We needed a plan that was BIGGER and BETTERER than Peach's, so everyone would vote for me to be Captain instead.

Here are some of the ideas we came up with.

# CAMPAIGN PLAN IDEAS AND CHANCES OF THEM WORKING

| Idea | Chance | Why/why not |
|---|---|---|
| Think up a really excellent campaign ~~slowgen~~ slogan.* | 10% | Slogans are really HARD. Especially when your name only rhymes with unhelpful words like umbrella and rubella. (Which is a medical sickness that gives you an itcherous red rash. Eww.) ☹ |

* A 'slogan' is some catchy, rhymerous words that make you want to buy something or vote for someone.

VOTE 1

UMBRELLA

RUBELLA (EWW.)

| | | |
|---|---|---|
| Give everyone free tickets to a Cassi Valentine concert. | 0% | She might be busy. And we don't even know her address. |
| Give everyone free triple-scoop ice-creams, in any flavour of their choice, with my slogan on the top. | 0% | We don't have any way to keep the ice-cream cold, so it would melt and make a BIG MESS everywhere which we would then have to clean up. Or any good slogans. |
| Lock Peach in a cupboard until the competition is over. | 0% | We tried this another time and it didn't work then either. |

| | | |
|---|---|---|
| Take down all Peach's posters and hide them where she will NEVER find them. | 25% | This one will only work if we don't get caught. Peach has eyes in the back of her head. And so do her friends, Prinny and Jade.       |
| Make lots of **BETTER** posters and stick them up around the school. | 100% | YESSSSS! This one is **BRILLIANT** to the power of a batrillion!!! Zoe and I are the Glitter Queens and extremely good at designing and making posters. |

First of all we tried writing some slogans.

Forget the rest – Ella's the BEST!

Don't be SHY. Give ELLA a try.

VOTE for ELLA. She's no Smeller.

This one was Olivia's.

Bleuchhh. These were all boring and hopelessly hopeless. Peach's slogan was a gazillion per cent betterer. ☹

So we decided to forget about snappy slogans and just put up powerful posters instead. Here are some we made:

Oceans ARE BLUE
Forests are Green
I'm the BEST PPC
That you've EVER seen!

VOTE 1 ELLa

HUG a TREE
with ME
VOTE 1 ELLA

DON'T
TRASH
YOUR
VOTE
VOTE 1 ELLA

Have to go to sleep now, Diary. Zoe and I are going to get to school SUPER early tomorrow morning so we can put my powerful posters up before anyone else* arrives.

* Especially YOU KNOW WHO.

Ella xoxo

## Friday, after school

Dear Diary,

### The Bad News

Zoe and I forgot to set our alarms. And we both slept in.

### The Good News

**Ha ha! only JOKING!**

Our alarms did go off! And we put all my posters up before anyone else arrived.

And guess where we put them?

Right next door to Pesky Princess Peach's posters. Hehehe.

And they looked aMAZing! Especially the HUG A TREE WITH ME one.

All these sweet little teensy tiny kids with sticky hands and snotty noses kept running up to me in the playground at little lunch and giving me giganterous, cuddly hugs.

Little TEENSY tiny KiD

Zoe says they will vote for me to be PPC for sure.

## The (For Real) Bad News

Chloe told me at the start of lunchtime that she saw my DON'T TRASH YOUR VOTE poster in the trash can.

I wonder how it got in there?

## The Badder News

Poppy and Georgia told me at the END of lunchtime that my other posters were in the bin as well. ☹☹

## The ~~Badderer~~ ~~Worserer~~ Worst News

Someone else in my class is campaigning to be Planet Protector Captain.

Raf.

He put up posters around the school too.

NOOOOOOOOO!

Raf is really, really, REALLY popular. All the boys will vote for him for sure.

And Peach and Prinny and Jade walked around the school today handing out chocolate cupcakes. With Pesky Peach's slogan piped on the top with minty green icing.

It's **SO NOT FAIR.** Why didn't I think of making cupcakes, instead of stupid melterous ice-cream?

**MY LIFE IS OVER.** I'm never going to be PPC now. Not in a million, gazillion, patrillion years.

Yours (in deep sorrow),

Ella ☹

## Friday, five minutes later (in less-deep sorrow)

I just **remembered** Something!

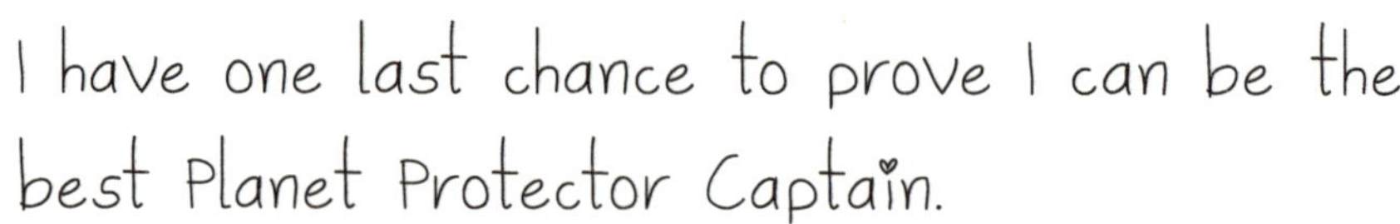

I have one last chance to prove I can be the best Planet Protector Captain.

On Monday, all the people who want to be PPC have to give a speech at assembly on a topic of their choice.

Ms Weiss told us this will be the **MOST** importerant part of our campaigns. Because we will be able to show off our ~~nolledge~~ ~~knollige~~ knowledge about our planet, and why we need to protect it, to the whole school.

**Yesssssss!**

I'm going to spend all weekend writing my speech. I can't wait!

E

## Sunday night, in bed

Dear Diary-doo,

Sorry I didn't write anything yesterday but I have been BUSY, BUSY, BUSY getting ready for my campaign speech tomorrow. I have decided to do it on whales.

## REASONS WHY I AM DOING WHALES FOR MY PPC SPEECH

1. Since I am also doing whales for my Endangered Animals of the World project, I already know pazillions of facts about them.

2 They are gentle (especially with their babies).

3 And smart (they know how to 'talk' to each other).

4 And gigantanterous!

5 Everyone loves whales.

6 They need our protection.

Zoe came over again today and we spent ALL morning making big presentation cards with whale pictures on them, and practising my speech.

And then after lunch we took Bob for a nice relaxing walk in the park.

And guess who we saw?

Precious Perfect Planet Protectorer Peach Parker. With her pesky friends, Prinny and Jade.

And guess what we saw Peach doing?

Feeding the ducks in the pond with bread. And she was standing right next to a sign that said not to do it!

My Nanna Kate told me you should NEVER EVER give bread to ducks.

Even if they come waddling up to you, wagging their sweet little duck tails, looking for food.

This is because bread is **VERY** bad for their tummies. And it makes them think they don't have to bother getting food for themselves because someone else will just bring it to them.

But the next thing Peach did was even ~~worserer~~ worse!

She threw her empty plastic water bottle on the ground. And left it there to roll away into the gutter. Even though she was **RIGHT NEXT TO** a recycling bin.

And then she walked off with a sneery smirk, like she was the boss of the whole planet and everything on it.

Nanna Kate never lets us drop things like bottles or plastic bags on the ground either. That bottle is going to roll down that gutter and into a drain and keep on rolling and rolling and rolling until—PLOP!—it rolls out into the sea. And then it will float around for bazillions of years in the water and maybe end up inside a baby dolphin's or even a baby whale's tummy.

Oh no! I had to save those poor baby dolphins and whales!

I immediately went into Top-Secret superhero mission mode. I sent a series of complicated hand signals to Zoe, telling her to pick up the bottle and meet me behind the nearest tree.

Zoe sent me a series of complicated hand signals back, telling me that she would.

Except something went wrong. And we ended up behind completely *different* trees.

So I sent her **ANOTHER** series of complicated hand signals that said, 'NOT that tree. THIS tree.'

And Zoe went, 'Oops!'

And I went, 'SSSSHHHHH!'

And Zoe went, 'Sorry!', only silently this time.

Then she tiptoed over on the tip of her tippy toes to join me.

We waited behind the tree until Peach and her friends walked past. Then we stealthily fell in behind them, shadowing their every move,

SUPERHero-Style.

Finally, I was able to put my Top-Secret superhero secret mission plan into action.

This is what happened next:

**Me** (bravely): Hey!

**Peach** (to Prinny, casually): Did you hear something?

**Prinny** (to Peach): Nope. How about you, Jade?

**Jade**: Nope. Must have been a park sloth.

*(Which is just silly. Anyone with even a tiny brain knows there are no sloths in our park.)*

**Me** (louder): Hey! Peach! I'm talking to you.

**Peach** (turning around smirkily): Oh. It's YOU. And your little friend.

**Prinny**: Yeah. What do YOU want?

**Me** (getting the bottle from Zoe and waving it at Peach): I think you dropped something?

**Peach**: Not me. Did you drop something, Prinny?

**Prinny**: Nope. Maybe it was the SLOTH.

**Zoe** (icily): It was so you. We saw you do it.

**Peach** (rolling her eyes): So what if I did?

**Prinny**: Yeah. So what?

**Jade**: Yeah. Why don't you mind your own beeswax, El-la?

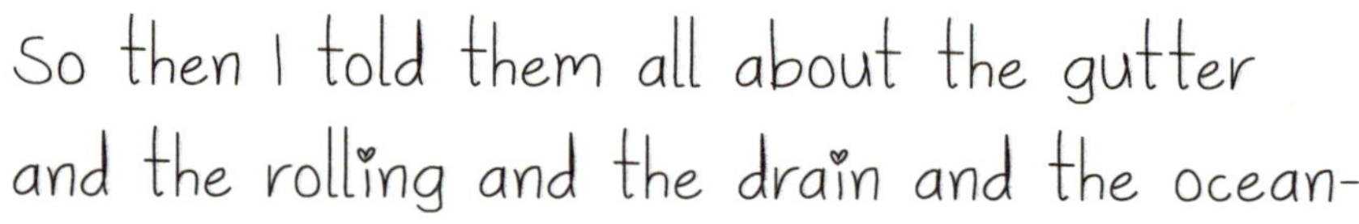

So then I told them all about the gutter and the rolling and the drain and the ocean-floating and the poor little baby whales' and dolphins' tummies. I figured if they knew what happened to baby whales and dolphins when you drop plastic rubbish on the ground they would be SHOCKED. Just like I was.

But guess what they said?

Peach (yawning): Have to go now. Our favourite celebrity TV show is starting soon.

Prinny: Yeah. We don't want to miss it.

Jade (waving): Yeah. Tootles!

Then they all turned around smirkily again and strutted away like matchy-matchy peacocks. So I walked over to the recycling bin and put the bottle in there MYSELF.

Peach makes me SO MAD, Diary! How can someone who doesn't even care about what happens to baby whales' tummies be the Planet Protector Captain?

AAAARRGGHH!

SO MAD

Yours 4 Ever,
Ella xx

## Monday, before dinner

Dear Diary,

I am in desperating despair to the power of 1000.

Today was the most **abominable**, **APPALLING**, **atrocious**, **AWFULLEST** day of my WHOLE LIFE! **EVER!**

Here's what happened.

We had our assembly, just like we always do on Monday mornings. Only this time the four kids who were trying out for PPC and giving speeches had to line up at the side of the stage. And then Mr Martini called out our names when it was our turn.

The first name he called was a girl from Grade 6 called Amity. Amity did her talk about joyful woodland creatures and how sad the world would be if we didn't have any. (You could tell she was really, really nerverous because her knees kept going **SHAKE, SHAKE, SHAKE** like a pair of shakerous maracas the whole time.)

At the end of her talk she played a very tragical and ~~mornful~~ mournful song on her recorder.

It was ~~a bit~~ VERY squeaky. I am not 100% sure if the squeaks were supposed to be the sounds that joyful woodland creatures make or if she was just too nerverous to play the right notes.

And then it was Raf's turn. As soon as Mr Martini said his name, Raf bounced out onto the stage. And guess what he was wearing?

A vampire costume! With a big, black cloak and a white face and giganterous fangs that dripped (fakerous) blood!

And guess what happened next? All his friends, like Peter and George and Billy and Zac and Tariq, came onto the stage wearing vampire outfits too! They ran around pretending to bite each other's necks and saying things like, 'I vant to drink your blood' and 'Fangs very much' to each other.

I vant to DRINK your BLOOD!

Fangs very MUCH!

And then Raf announced that he was going to do a serious rap song he'd written about something called a VAMPIRE LOAD.* And how the planet needed to be protected from it.

* A vampire load is when you leave a thing like a TV or computer or a microwave switched on at the power point all the time, even when you're not ~~acksherly~~ actually using it. That DRAINS the power, just like a vampire DRAINS blood when he bites someone with his biterous fangs.

This is how Raf's rap song went:

Vam-pire load! Vam-pire load!
Pull the plug,
Don't be a toad!

Are you using too much power?
Wasting energy every hour?
TVs, chargers, cordless phones,
All these things live
In your homes.

Vam-pire load! Vam-pire load!
Pull the plug,
Don't be a toad!

ZOW-ee! Raf's rap was excellent. And clever. And fantabulously fabulous! Everyone was smiling and clapping their hands and singing along with him.

Even Ms Weiss clapped (which is weird, because normally she's telling him to sit down and stop being such a noisy trouble-maker).

CLAP!

CLAP!

CLAP!

And then he sang the next bit:

*Fire alarms and*
*Video games—*
*Stop wasting energy*
*Use your BRAINS!*

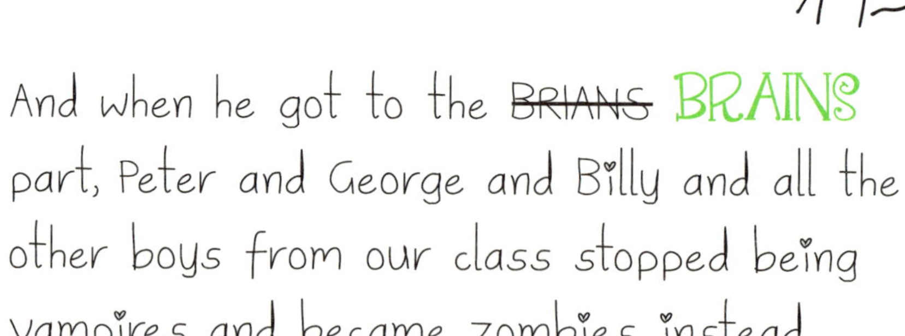

And when he got to the ~~BRIANS~~ BRAINS part, Peter and George and Billy and all the other boys from our class stopped being vampires and became zombies instead.

Brains

And they walked around the stage with their arms straight out in front of them and their eyes rolling back in their heads, going, 'BRAI-I-I-I-NNNNS!'

BRAINS

Then all of a sudden other boys in the audience (even some teeny tiny ones) jumped up out of their seats. And then Raf called out for everyone to join in and whooped them all up until LOADS of kids were running around the hall waving their arms and screeching, 'BRAINS! BRA-I-I-I-NNNNNS!' too.

It was like one big, giganterous zombie-fest!

And then Mr Martini and Mrs Sneed (our assistant principal) started waving their arms around and screeching as well. Only they weren't saying, 'BRA-I-I-I-NNNNNS!' They were saying, 'Stop that nonsense and SIT DOWN NOW!!!'

Boys. They are such BIG BABIES.

Mr Martini waited until all the kids had stopped arm-wavering and eye-rollering and were sitting quietly in their seats again.

Then he called out my name and I came to the front and did my speech. And it was aMAZing! Much better than I thought it was going to be. ☺

## REASONS WHY MY SPEECH WAS AMAZING:

1. I didn't forget any of my words. ✔

My knees didn't shake like shakerous maracas like Amity's did. ✔

3 I showed everyone the cards I made with the pictures of the gentle, smart, giganterous whales on them. And I only dropped one of them. ✔

4 Everyone clapped at the end. ✔

CLAP
CLAP
CLAP

5 Some people (like Zoe and Amethyst and Cordelia) even CHEERED. ✔

I ran back to my seat and Zoe looked at me with shiny eyes. And then she gave me a giganterous hug. And I looked back at Zoe with even shinier eyes.

Maybe people liked my speech enough to vote for me! ☺☺☺

I was just planning my outfit for when I'm invited to Parliament House to accept an award for Excellence in Planet Protection when something horrendously horrible happened.

Mr Martini called out Peach's name. And she came out to the front of the stage and did her speech. And all my hopes and dreams of being the PPC went POP! and slipped sadly away down the drain like the bubblous bubbles in a bubble bath when you pull the plug out.

Because guess what she did her PPC speech on?

HINT: It rhymes with tail

Have to go now, Diary. Dad's calling me for dinner. We're having homemade pizza. I hope I won't be too distraught to eat it. ☹

HomeMade PIZZA YUM!

## Monday night, after dinner

Hey there, Diary,

I'm back!

So, here is the part where I tell you what Peach did her PPC speech on.

The answer is . . .

DRUM ROLL

Can you believe it?

She **COPIED** me. **AGAIN**.

Only Peach didn't just do a talk and hold up presentation cards with picture of whales on them, like I did.

She showed sad whale pictures on a big screen while she was doing her speech.

And sad and tragical sounds of lonely whales calling to each other came out through the loud speakers at the side of the stage.

Like this:

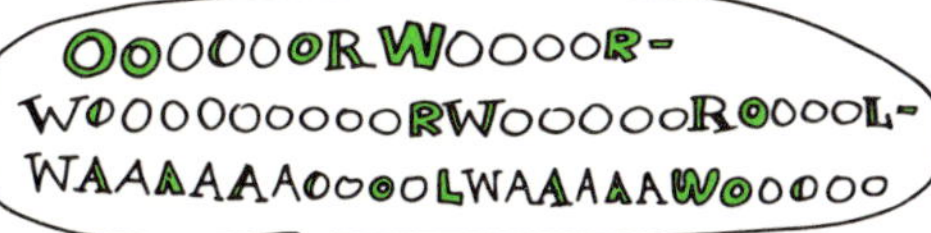

And then Prinny and Jade and four of their fancy gym-bun friends came out onto the stage wearing grey T-shirts and black leggings and did a sad whale dance, with lots of sad arm fluttering and twirling pirouettes.

And then another two of her friends climbed up onto the stage holding a giganterous banner that said:

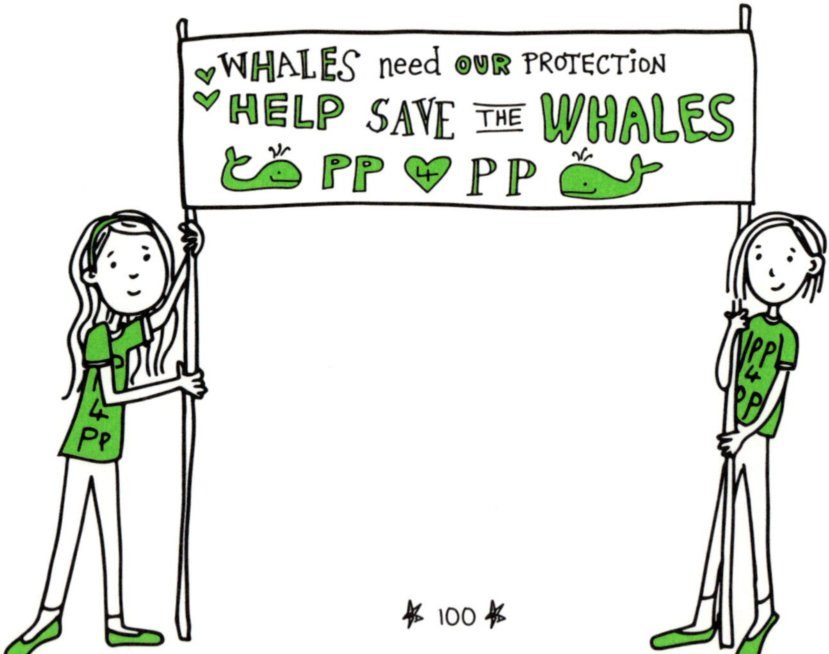

WHALES need OUR PROTECTION
HELP SAVE THE WHALES
PP 4 PP

And everyone clapped AND cheered. Some of the teensy tiny little kids even cried.

It is SO not fair, Diary. I really, really, really, really, really, really, really (to the power of infinity x 1000) want to be the Planet Protector Captain. And now everyone is going to vote for Pesky Princess Peach Parker for sure.

Yours in desperating despair,
Ella ☹

## VOTING INSTRUCTIONS

Place a tick in the box next to the student you think would make the best **Planet PROTECTOR CAPTAIN**

☐ Amity

~~☐ Raf~~

☐ ELLA

☐ Peach

Raf got into **BIG TROUBLE** with Mr Martini and Mrs Sneed for being a trouble-maker. So now he has been disqualified.

## Tuesday, after school

Waiting to get the results.

## Wednesday, before dinner

Still waiting.

My cold and unfeeling family haven't even bothered to ask me why I have been so pale and distraught lately.

## Thursday, after dinner (which I barely touched)

STILL WAITING

Still waiting.

(Maybe something 'unexpected' will happen, like Peach's house getting flooded by a ~~soonarmy~~ ~~stunarmy~~ ~~tsunarmi~~ big wave which means her family has to move to her aunt's place in Timbuktooty for the rest of the year, and she'll get disqualified as well.)

## Friday night, in bed

Dearest Diary,

Mr Martini announced the PPC voting results over the loudspeakers at the start of lunchtime today.

### The Bad News

I didn't win.

### The Badder News

Peach did.

## The Not-So-Bad News

One of the other campaigning people got almost as many votes as Peach. So Mr Martini decided to make a special brand-new job called Planet Protector VICE-Captain (PPVC).

## The Good News

It's me!

Ella! I'm the PPVC!

YESSSSSSS!

Ms Weiss told Peach and me that she was **exTREMEly** proud that both the PPC and the PPVC had come from her class.

And that she was going to organise some special times each week for us to work together on our planet protecting projects. Starting straightaway right now.

Peach looked around royally (again). Only this time she made a fakey speech all about how honoured she was to be working with someone who cared as much about our wonderful planet as she did.

And Ms Weiss smiled her special award-giving smile and wrote her name up on the **STUDENT STARS** section of the board **AGAIN**, for displaying 'strong leadership skills'.

**BLEUCHHH!**

Then she made Zoe and Prinny and Jade move to another table so that Peach and I could sit TOGETHER.

Ms Weiss gave us a special book that said PLANET PROTECTORS in fancy writing on the cover. And on the very first page was a list of all the different jobs we had to do.

## List of PP Captain and Vice-Captain Responsibilities (to be shared out equally)

1. Weed garden beds.

2. Plant native trees to attract birds.

3. Clean out the worm farm.

4. Shovel chook poo on to garden beds.

5. Count number of ice-cream wrappers in canteen bin.

6. Remove any scrunchable plastic from the recycling bins.

7. Give talks and announce results at assembly wearing PP superhero outfit.

8. Count the number of nude food lunches in each classroom.

And guess what happened next? You never ever will in a million pazillion years so I'll just tell you.

Peach (smiling sweetly): Um, Ella?

Smiling Sweetly

Me (suspiciously): Yes?

Peach: There's something I've been meaning to tell you for AGES.

Me (checking my back with my hand to make sure Peter or Raf hadn't stuck any sticky notes there that had rude words on them. Which they ~~sometimes~~ often do. They hadn't): Oh?

**Peach**: I really, really, REALLY like your style. You know, your outfits and stuff. And so do Prinny and Jade.

**Me** (shocked): You do?

**Peach** (leaning in close): Truly-ruly, cross my heart hope to die. You're SOOO stylish and designerish. You could be a fashion designer.

**Me** (glowing): ☺

**Peach** (casually): So anyway, you know how we have to divide up all the jobs?

**Me** (nodding)

**Peach**: Well, one of the jobs is REALLY hard.

**Me** (puzzled): Which one?

Peach: The superhero one. You have to give a really tricky talk at assembly. In a superhero outfit. Where are we going to get one of those?

Me (thrilled): I could make one! It will be easy-peasy. Zow-ee. I've always wanted to be a superhero.

Peach (smiling sweetly): You're the best.

Me: ☺☺☺

Have to stop writing soon, Diary. I'm getting up super early tomorrow morning so I can start making my superhero outfit.

I was secretly working on designs for it when I was supposed to be writing a report on what the Ancient Egyptians ate back in their ancient olden days. (Not very much. They didn't even have pizza. Or spag bol! Bleuchhh.)

It is going to be aMAZing. And EXcellent. And fantabulously fabulously FABulous!

Sweet dreams.

Yours 4 ever,

Ella xoxo

## Sunday night, after dinner

Dearest, darlingest Diary,

I spent ALL weekend working on my superhero outfit and speech for my very first Planet Protectors assembly.

Zoe came over yesterday for an EOMM (Emergency Outfit-Making Meeting). This time I made sure Olivia didn't try any of her sneaky tricks to get inside my room by gluing strips of cardboard over the cracks between the door and the door frame part.

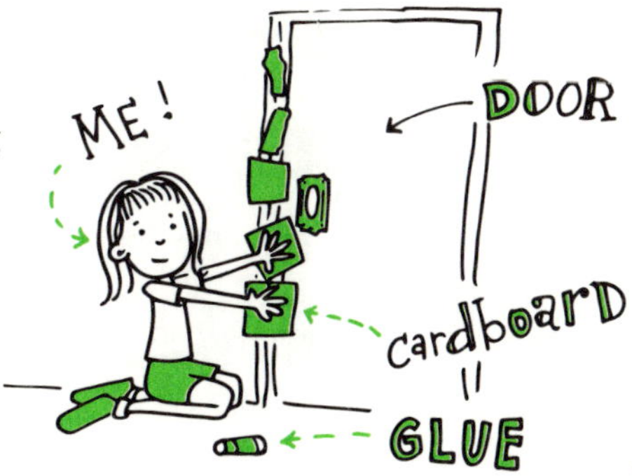

~~Unforch~~ Unfortunately that meant we couldn't get out, either. ☹ (Fortunately I had made extra snacks or we might have died a sad and tragical death from starverisation.)

Here are some of our early designs:

We also designed some fantabulous outfits for Bob, just for fun. I wish he could come to school with me. He'd make an excellent superhero companion!

And here is the final, finished superhero outfit! Nanna Kate took us to Fancy Fine Fabric Fair so we could get all the special shimmery, shiny materials we needed to make it.

I LOVE it. I am going to look specTACular. And stuPENDous! And senSATional!

I can't wait to show Peach tomorrow morning!!!

Yours 4 ever,
Ella x

## Monday, after school

Dear Diary,

I am SHOCKED.

(Again.)

E

## Monday, about two minutes later

Why does Peach always have to be so mean?

EsPECially to ME? "WHY?

WHY? WHY? Why!?

## Monday, about two minutes after that

**Monday, about another two minutes after that**

**Monday, about forty-five minutes later (after a nice relaxing walk in the park with Bob)**

OK, here's what happened.

Zoe and I arrived at school super-duper early. This was so she could help me get changed into my spectacular superhero outfit before all the other kids came rushing into the hall for our very first Planet Protectors assembly. We were so **EXCITERATED** we were (almost) jumping out of our skins!

Especially as we'd been practising my special superhero entrance **ALL WEEKEND**.

First of all, Zoe was going to come out onto the dark stage dressed all in black (so you couldn't see her).

And then she was going to say (in a spooky voice):

Is that the Rain?

**(VICE)-CAPTAIN PLANET PROTECTOR!**

And then an extremely bright spotlight would go **FLASH!** in the middle of the stage.

And special superhero music we found in Dad's ancient CD collection would start playing.

And I'd come rushing across from the side of the stage like a rushing wind and stand right in the middle of the spotlight's glowing ring.

And all the kids in the audience would go,

'OOOOOOOOOoooOOoo!!'

(Especially all the little teeny tiny ones in the front row.)

Then I was going to give an extremely serious speech about why you should NEVER:

★ Trample all over the flower beds in the playground, even if you are chasing a runaway bouncy ball.

TRAMPLED flower BED

♡ Waste precious water when you are drinking from the bubblers by letting it drip everywhere.

DRINKING BUBBLER

- Bring food to school that is all wrapped up in plastic packaging.



- Leave litter lying around in the playground, in case it rolls down the drain and out into the ocean where it could hurt dolphins and sea turtles and baby whales.

- Hurt or step on little creatures when you're running around the playground or in your garden.



And then right at the very end I was going to shake my finger at the little kids and say, in a deeperous superhero voice:

Only guess what happened?

I didn't get to wear my superhero outfit. (Not even the scrunchie.)

Or come rushing onto the stage like a rushing wind.

Or make my serious speech.

Or say, 'I'll be watching you' at the end to the little kids in the front row.

# PEACH DID!!!

CHEATEROUS TRICKSTER!!!

Because she is a cheaterous trickster. Just like my little sister, Olivia. Only worse.

Peach was **NEVER** going to let me do that speech. She only wanted me to make the superhero outfit so she could take it off me and wear it **HERSELF!**

## Tuesday, after school

Guess what I did at lunchtime today?

Counted all the icky sticky ice-cream wrappers in the canteen rubbish bin. Now I have stinky pinkies.

Eww.

## Wednesday, before dinner

And guess what I did at lunchtime today?

Cleaned out the worm farm and shovelled chook poo. Now my pinkies are even stinkier.

Shovel
CHOOK
POO

Double eww.

## Wednesday, after dinner

And guess what I'll probably be doing at lunchtime tomorrow? And every lunchtime for the rest of the term?

Climbing into the very bottomest part of the recycling bin to separate all the scruncherous chip bags and biscuit wrappers from the un-scruncherous rubbish, so they can go to a special place to get melted down and made into sweet little outdoor tables and chairs.

All because Princess Picky Peach Parker doesn't like getting her precious, perfect hands dirty.

ME

Yours in
desperation,
Ella

**Thursday, after school**

Dear Diary,

You will NEVER, EVER, EVER be able to guess what happened today.

Precious Princess Peach was inspecting one of the garden beds.

And there was a giganterous swarm of sweet little ladybirds, swarming all over the branch part of a rose bush.

And Peach saw them. And she screamed. Like this:

And guess what? The ladybirds didn't fly away home. They just stayed right where they were, swarming swarmerously.

And Peach ran into the office and came back with a giganterous can of bug spray. She was about to squirt it all over the sweet little ladybirds when Zoe stopped her, just in time to save them.

It's so not fair, Diary. Peach Parker is the ~~worsterest~~ worst Planet Protector Captain in the history of Planet Protector Captains!

We have to do something!

Ella

XOXO

## Thursday, about half an hour later

Dear Diary,

I've thought of a way to try and get Peach to be a better PPC!

Zoe is coming over soon so we can have an emergency Emergency Meeting about it.

My plan is going to be **BRILLIANT!**

Talk soon, Diary.

E xx

## Friday night, in bed

Dearest Diary,

As soon as we arrived at school today, Zoe and I went into Top-Secret superhero spy mode. I had my Top-Secret secret detective notebook with me (and Dad's old binoculars) so we could (super sneakily) **COLLECT EVIDENCE** of all the ways Peach was being the **WORST PPC EVER!**

We followed Peach's every move at recess and lunchtime. Here are some of the rotten, atrocious, despicably despicable things we saw her doing.

1. Trampling the flowers we planted when she was taking a shortcut to get to the canteen so she could be first in line.

Trampled FLOWERS

2. Snapping a low branch off everyone's favourite tree in the playground because it scratched her arm when she was running past it. And there was a teeny tiny little lizard on the branch! ☹

3. Casually throwing an empty chip packet on the ground.

4. Eating a fancy lunch with lots of scruncherous plastic packaging. And not even putting it in the scruncherous plastic recycling bin when she'd finished!

5. Leaving the tap running in the girls' toilets while she was talking to Prinny and Jade.

**ALL** of the things I was going to tell the school **NOT** to do in my superhero speech!

So then we showed Peach all our evidence we had collected in my notebook. And we said if she didn't start being a proper Planet Protector Captain, we'd show it to Ms Weiss. And maybe even Mr Martini.

But Peach just tossed her perfect ponytail and said,



And then she strutted off with Prinny and Jade.

Maybe my brilliant plan wasn't so brilliant after all. ☹☹☹

## Friday night, ten minutes later

I forgot to tell you about an EXcellent thing that *did* happen today!

This afternoon, Ms Weiss announced to the WHOLE CLASS that she had noticed all the cleaning and the shovelling and the scruncherous plastic sorting in the rubbish bins I had been doing.

Then she gave me TWO Student Stars on the board for being a valuable Vice-Captain and also for my 'outstanding commitment to the PPP'. Yay!

## PS (three days later)

Guess what?!

Today Peach told Ms Weiss that she doesn't want to be Planet Protector Captain anymore, because her famous opera-singing aunt from Timbuktooty was coming to stay. And she was going to be too busy having opera-singing lessons with her to do any more Planet Protectering.

And guess who the new Planet Protector Captain and Vice-Captain are now?

Read more of Ella's brilliant diary in

and look out for more coming soon!